Tatton Mere
The Moor
Booths Hall
King Street
Brook St.
Toft Road
Knutsford 1750's
Tatton Hall
Princess Street.
Warrington Road
(The Grandstand)
Tabley Road
The Heath (Races)
Tabley Lane
Heathside
Toft Hall
Heath House
Love Lane
Tabley Hall
Higgins Hit-list
Tatton Hall
Tabley Hall
Booths Hall
Toft Hall

To Knutsford!

Edward Higgins Esquire winced as the wheel on the 10 O'Clock coach from Liverpool hit yet another jolting rut in the road. The sooner he reached Knutsford, the better for his back, and Knutsford's two streets had plenty of good inns and coaching houses, including The George and The Angel.

But it was Knutsford Races that really piqued Higgins' interest. Haughty gentlemen and pretty ladies paraded in all their finery while the jostling, thundering animals charged around The Heath on the edge of town.

Knutsford Races on The Heath

The races held great prospects for Higgins. Wagering on the horses, crowding round the noisy, screeching cock-pit or picking out his favourite man at the boxing. Most of all though, Higgins needed to make friends – rich friends who would unknowingly fund his extravagancies.

And what a time he had! With his easy charm and carefree spending, Higgins was soon firm friends with all the local gentry...Leycester and Leicester, the Leghs and, of course, Mr Samuel Egerton, Lord of the Manor and the richest of them all.

At The George

"Why don't you stay?", suggested Lord Egerton over a drink after the final race was done. "Heath House has come to let. I'll introduce you to Mr Skellorn, the owner. I'm sure he would be agreeable to you taking the place. It's old, but has fine stables."

Higgins couldn't believe his luck and with a straight face said "Why, what an idea! I suppose I could".

Soon it was settled and Higgins was installed in Heath House. What a commotion! A new gentleman in town, with three fine horses in his stables, pockets of gold…and a bachelor as well!

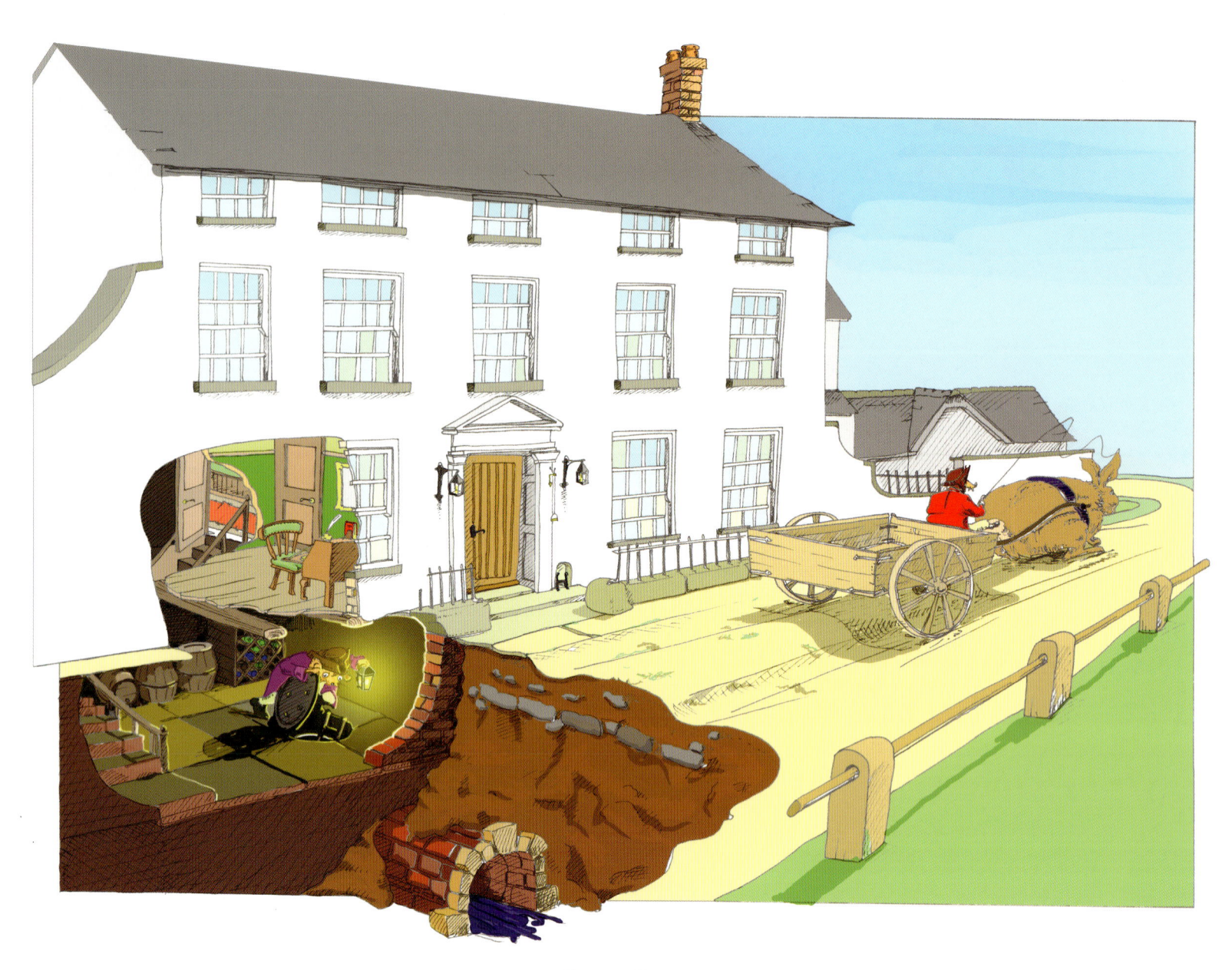

Heath House

Heath House proved to be a revelation, especially when Higgins discovered the grate in the cellar that led to an old drain that ran under the house and out toward The Heath.

"And a secret tunnel. Well, well, Knutsford really is the place to be!"

Courting by the river

One sunny afternoon Higgins was riding along Top Street, looking the very picture of respectability, when he stopped to let a pretty young lady pass on the narrow street. "Good afternoon. I don't believe we have met. My name is Higgins and I'm new to the town." The young lady curtseyed and introduced herself as Miss Birtles of King Street.

From that day on the couple were often seen walking along the small river that ran from Sanctuary Moor, past Brook House, over the ford and on through town. So nobody was surprised when their engagement was announced.

Stealing the Cup

Weddings are expensive though, and Highwayman Higgins was not inclined to spend his own money. It was time for a little "shopping".

Scandal hit town shortly after when the Knutsford Race Day Winner's Silver Cup was stolen from the meeting rooms above The George. And when Mr Legh's favourite silver snuffbox was taken from his dressing room, people remarked how outraged Higgins was to hear about the misfortune that had befallen his good friend.

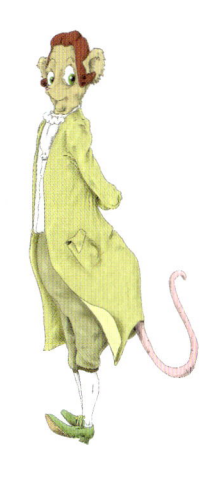

Another bill

The wedding came and went, and Heath House was to be given a fresh coat of white paint and new furniture too.
The new Mrs Higgins delighted in ordering all the latest styles from London and no expense was spared, much to Higgins' dismay.

"But surely we can afford it Edward?", Mrs Higgins enquired as he opened yet another bill.

"Of course dear, of course", he said through gritted teeth. "Which reminds me, I have a little business to attend to this evening – you will have to dine without me." That same night, his friend, Lord Egerton, was relieved of a large sum of money that was hidden in his writing desk!

Out in the town

Good news, however, was to follow. Everyone in town was pleased when they heard that Mrs Higgins was expecting a baby and soon Heath House was filled with the noise and laughter of the young Higgins family.

But children are expensive, and as time passed, Highwayman Higgins was becoming desperate.

Then, Mr Leycester of Toft Hall had his handsome lock-box taken with Mrs Leycester's jewellery inside it. And one night Mr Leicester of Tabley Hall, heard a noise and came down the stairs to see a figure in black running down the drive. The miscreant was never found, but half a key was discovered, broken off in the lock of the family safe.

Call the constables

"These last ten years have been a plague of crime", said Lord Egerton. "In fact, the only person who has not been robbed is Higgins!"

"Hmmm", said Leycester thoughtfully.
"Interesting", said Legh. And then the penny dropped.

"Higgins!", they all shouted together.

"Never! I don't believe it! The bounder! I'm calling the constables! This is an abomination!", spluttered an apoplectic Lord Egerton.

Escape through the tunnel